Table of Contents

My Shadow,
page 9

Beaches Wall Hanging,
page 22

Nightfire Bed Runner,
page 19

Introduction

It Takes Three contains quilt tops you can make with only three yards of fabrics. These quilts have style and great design. If you're looking for a fun, quick and easy project for a friend or maybe for a charity quilt, here's where you'll find it. Each project in this book is constructed using only three yards of fabric to complete the top, excluding binding and backing.

In many cases, you'll be able to pull together enough fabrics from your stash to complete an entire quilt. Because some of these projects would be perfect for charity quilts, consider the possibility of using fabrics you have on hand to make someone else a special, much-needed gift. If you're looking for a great idea book with fabulous and versatile patterns, look no further—you've just found it.

Any way you look at it, these eight quilt projects are treasures. Enjoy!

Estimating Yardage

When using yardage, we use a 42" width from selvage to selvage to compute the number of strips or pieces to be cut for our patterns. When using fat quarters, we use 18" x 21" for these computations.

It is always best to purchase a little extra fabric to allow for shrinkage if you prewash your fabrics and to allow for straightening fabrics before the first cut and again during cutting if more than eight strips are cut from one fabric.

Appian Way Bed Runner

This traditional design makes piecing and fabric selection easy.
Make this runner to add a touch of excitement to your bed.

Designed & Quilted by Julie Weaver

Skill Level

Confident Beginner

Project Note

The yardages listed include just a little extra fabric for straightening. We advise you to purchase extra to allow for straightening your fabric before and during the cutting process if your fabric supplier does not do so when cutting your yardage.

Specifications

Bed Runner Size: 72" x 30"
Block Size: 10" x 10" finished
Number of Blocks: 12

Materials

- ½ yard red print
- ⅝ yard binding fabric
- ¾ yard green print
- ¾ yard dark blue floral
- 1 yard cream print
- Backing to size
- Batting to size
- Thread
- Basic sewing tools and supplies

Appian Way
10" x 10" Finished Block
Make 12

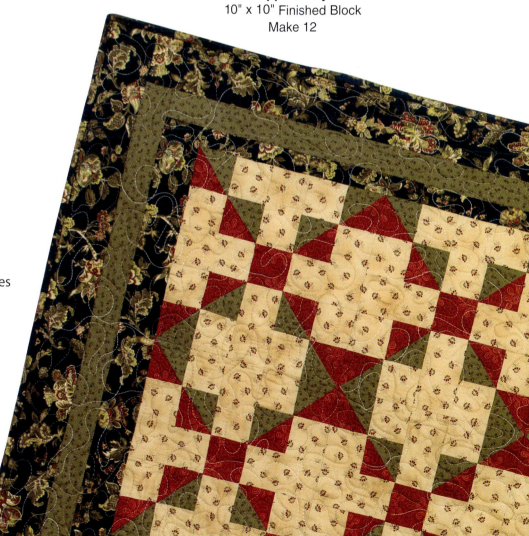

Cutting

From red print:
- Cut 1 (2½" by fabric width) strip.
  Subcut strip into 12 (2½") A squares.
- Cut 4 (2⅞" by fabric width) strips.
  Subcut strips into 48 (2⅞") B squares.

From binding fabric:
- Cut 6 (2¼" by fabric width) binding strips.

From green print:
- Cut 4 (2⅞" by fabric width) strips.
  Subcut strips into 48 (2⅞") C squares.
- Cut 5 (2" by fabric width) H/I strips.

From dark blue floral:
- Cut 3 (1½" by fabric width) F strips.
- Cut 2 (2½" by fabric width) strips.
  Trim strips to make 2 (2½" x 22½") G strips.
- Cut 5 (3" by fabric width) J/K strips.

From cream print:
- Cut 6 (2½" by fabric width) strips.
  Subcut strips into 96 (2½") D squares.
- Cut 3 (4½" by fabric width) strips.
  Subcut strips into 48 (2½" x 4½") E rectangles.

Inspiration

"Tradition was the inspiration for this quilt. The fabric I chose is reminiscent of the 1860–1890 time period, and the design is pretty traditional too. We, as quilters, carry on old traditions and create new ones in each and every quilt we make. We need to celebrate these traditions."

—Julie Weaver

Completing the Blocks

1. Draw a diagonal line from corner to corner on the wrong side of each B square.

2. Referring to Figure 1, place a C square right sides together with a B square and stitch ¼" on each side of the marked line. Cut apart on the marked line and press open to make two B-C units. Repeat to make a total of 96 B-C units.

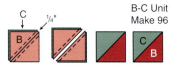

Figure 1

3. To complete one Appian Way block, select one A square, four E rectangles and eight each D squares and B-C units.

4. Sew a B-C unit to a D square with the C side next to D to make a B-C-D unit as shown in Figure 2; press. Repeat with the D square next to B to complete a D-B-C unit, again referring to Figure 2.

Figure 2

5. Join the units pieced in step 4 to complete a corner unit as shown in Figure 3; press. Repeat to make a total of four corner units.

Figure 3

6. Join two corner units with an E rectangle to make the top row as shown in Figure 4; press. Repeat to make the bottom row.

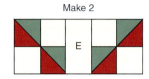

Make 2

Figure 4

7. Sew the A square between two E rectangles to complete the center row as shown in Figure 5; press.

Figure 5

8. Sew the center row between the top and bottom rows to complete one Appian Way block as shown in Figure 6; press.

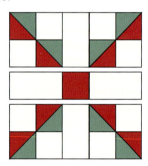

Figure 6

9. Repeat steps 3–8 to complete a total of 12 Appian Way blocks.

Completing the Bed Runner

Refer to the Assembly Diagram for positioning of pieces for all steps.

1. Join six blocks to make a block row; press. Repeat to make a second block row.

2. Join the block rows to complete the bed runner center; press.

3. Join the F strips on the short ends to make a long strip; press. Subcut strip into two 1½" x 60½" F strips.

4. Sew F strips to opposite long sides and the G strips to the short ends of the bed runner center; press.

5. Join the H/I strips on the short ends to make a long strip; press. Subcut strip into two each 2" x 64½" H strips and 2" x 25½" I strips.

6. Sew H strips to opposite long sides and I strips to the short ends of the bed runner center; press.

7. Join the J/K strips on the short ends to make a long strip; press. Subcut strip into two each 3" x 67½" J strips and 3" x 30½" K strips.

8. Sew J strips to opposite long sides and K strips to the short ends of the bed runner center to complete the top; press.

9. Create a quilt sandwich referring to Quilting Basics on page 44.

10. Quilt as desired.

11. Bind referring to Quilting Basics on page 44 to finish. ●

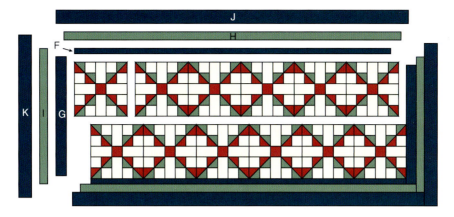

Appian Way Bed Runner
Assembly Diagram 72" x 30"

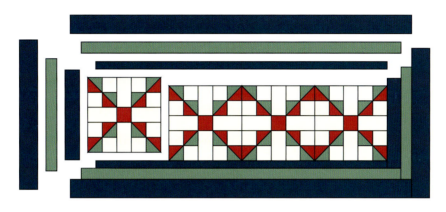

Appian Way Table Runner
Alternate-Size Assembly Diagram 52" x 20"
Just use 1 row of 4 blocks to make a table runner.

Here's a Tip

When sewing heavily seamed blocks together, as in this project, try to lock the seams as often as possible to make the sewing process easier and less stressful. Sometimes that means pressing a seam one way, and then clipping into the seam to press it another way to lock the seam later (Figures A and B).

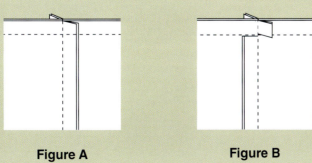

Figure A   **Figure B**

My Shadow

It's amazing what you can do with just three yards of fabric and a fun design. This lap quilt would be a perfect project to clear out your stash.

Designed & Quilted by Julie Weaver

Skill Level
Confident Beginner

Project Note
The yardages listed include just a little extra fabric for straightening. We advise you to purchase extra to allow for straightening your fabric before and during the cutting process if your fabric supplier does not do so when cutting your yardage.

Specifications
Quilt Size: 42" x 48"
Block Size: 6" x 6" finished
Number of Blocks: 30

Materials
- ⅜ yard light plum print
- ⅜ yard medium plum print
- ½ yard binding fabric
- ¾ yard dark plum print
- ¾ yard cream small floral
- ¾ yard cream large floral
- Backing to size
- Batting to size
- Thread
- Basic sewing tools and supplies

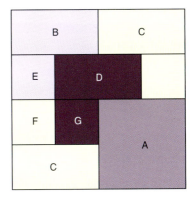

Shadow
6" x 6" Finished Block
Make 30

Cutting

From light plum print:
- Cut 2 (3½" by fabric width) B strips.
- Cut 2 (2" by fabric width) E strips.

From medium plum print:
- Cut 3 (3½" by fabric width) strips.
  Subcut strips into 30 (3½") A squares.

From binding fabric:
- Cut 5 (2¼" by fabric width) binding strips.

From dark plum print:
- Cut 2 (3½" by fabric width) D strips.
- Cut 2 (2" by fabric width) G strips.
- Cut 8 (1½" by fabric width) strips.
  Trim strips to make 2 strips each 1½" x 36½" H,
  1½" x 32½" I, 1½" x 41½" L and 1½" x 37½" M.

From cream small floral:

- Cut 4 (3½" by fabric width) C strips.
    Subcut 2 strips into 30 (2" x 3½") C rectangles.
- Cut 4 (2" by fabric width) F strips.

From cream large floral:

- Cut 4 (2" by fabric width) strips.
    Trim strips to make 2 (2" x 38½") J strips
        and 2 (2" x 35½") K strips.
- Cut 5 (3" by fabric width) N/O strips.

Completing the Blocks

1. Sew a B strip to a C strip along length to make a B-C strip set; press. Repeat to make a second strip set.

2. Subcut the B-C strip sets into 30 (2" x 6½") B-C segments as shown in Figure 1.

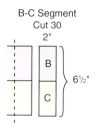

B-C Segment
Cut 30

Figure 1

3. Sew a D strip between an E strip and an F strip along length to make an E-D-F strip set; press. Repeat to make a second strip set.

4. Subcut the E-D-F strip sets into 30 (2" x 6½") E-D-F segments as shown in Figure 2.

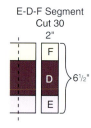

E-D-F Segment
Cut 30

Figure 2

Inspiration

"The block was the inspiration for this quilt. You can do lots of things with this particular block simply by rearranging the fabrics and turning the block when assembling the quilt. I really like the way the traditional use of light, medium and dark fabrics creates a stacked effect."

—*Julie Weaver*

5. Sew an F strip to a G strip along length to make an F-G strip set; press. Repeat to make a second strip set.

6. Subcut the F-G strip sets into 30 (2" x 3½") F-G segments as shown in Figure 3.

F-G Segment
Cut 30

Figure 3

7. To complete one Shadow block, select one each A square, C rectangle and B-C, E-D-F and F-G segment.

8. Sew the C rectangle to the F-G segment to make a corner unit as shown in Figure 4; press.

Figure 4

9. Sew A to the corner unit as shown in Figure 5; press.

Figure 5

10. Sew the B-C segment to the E-D-F segment as shown in Figure 6; press.

Figure 6

11. Join the two pieced units as shown in Figure 7 to complete one Shadow block; press.

Figure 7

12. Repeat steps 7–11 to complete a total of 30 Shadow blocks.

Completing the Quilt

Refer to the Assembly Diagram for positioning of pieces for all steps.

1. Arrange and join five Shadow blocks to make a row; repeat to make six rows. ***Note:*** *Be careful of the placement of the blocks in the rows. Blocks must be placed a specific way to form the secondary design at the corners where the A squares meet in the rows.*

2. Join the rows to complete the quilt center; press.

3. Sew H strips to opposite long sides and I strips to the top and bottom of the quilt center; press.

4. Repeat step 3 with J, K, L and M strips.

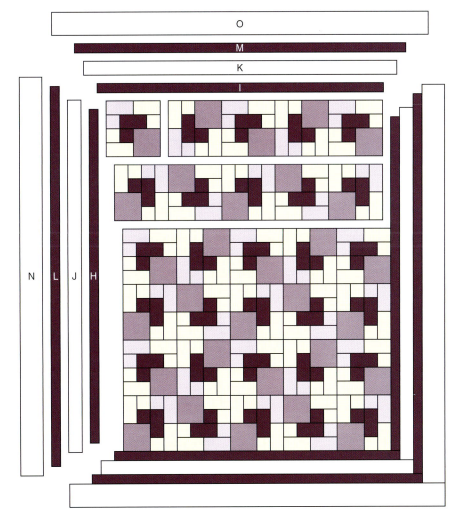

My Shadow
Assembly Diagram 42" x 48"

5. Join the N/O strips on the short ends to make a long strip; press. Subcut strip into two each 3" x 43½" N strips and 3" x 42½" O strips.

6. Sew the N strips to opposite long sides and O strips to the top and bottom of the bordered quilt center to complete the quilt top; press.

7. Create a quilt sandwich referring to Quilting Basics on page 44.

8. Quilt as desired.

9. Bind referring to Quilting Basics on page 44 to finish. ●

Here's a Tip

Making strip-pieced units allows you to piece these blocks quickly.

Taking the time to figure out which way to press seams in order to make the blocks go together easily ultimately makes the quilt assembly much easier and almost eliminates ripping apart seams to change pressing direction.

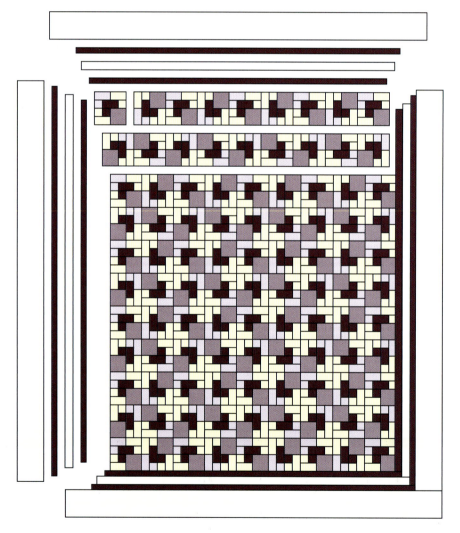

My Shadow
Alternate-Size Assembly Diagram 71" x 83"
Add 4 blocks to the width and 5 blocks to the length and increase the size
of the outer border strips to finish at 5" to make a twin-size quilt.

How Does Your Garden Grow?

This quick and easy quilt has lots of possibilities. Change the focus fabric and you can easily change the theme of the quilt.

Designed & Quilted by Julie Weaver

Skill Level
Beginner

Project Note
Some of the yardages listed include just a little extra fabric for straightening. We advise you to purchase extra to allow for straightening your fabric before and during the cutting process if your fabric supplier does not do so when cutting your yardage.

Specifications
Quilt Size: 48" x 53"

Materials
- ½ yard yellow dots
- ½ yard cream/gray dots
- ½ yard gray tonal
- ⅝ yard binding fabric
- 1½ yards gray floral
- Backing to size
- Batting to size
- Thread
- Basic sewing tools and supplies

Cutting

From yellow dots:
- Cut 6 (2¼" by fabric width) strips.

From cream/gray dots:
- Cut 6 (2¼" by fabric width) strips.

From gray tonal:
- Cut 4 (2" by fabric width) strips.
  Trim strips to make 2 (2" x 40½") F strips and 2 (2" x 38½") G strips.
- Cut 5 (1½" by fabric width) J/K strips.

From binding fabric:
- Cut 6 (2¼" by fabric width) binding strips.

From gray floral:
- Cut 2 (5½" by fabric width) strips.
  Subcut strips into 14 (5½") A squares.
- Cut 6 (2" by fabric width) strips.
- Cut 5 (4½" by fabric width) H/I strips.

Here's a Tip
Make the strip sets, and then cut and assemble the quilt center one vertical row at a time to avoid confusion.

Completing the Quilt

Refer to the Assembly Diagram for positioning of pieces for steps 3–9.

1. Sew a 2"-wide gray floral strip between one each 2¼"-wide cream/gray dots and yellow dots strip along length to make a strip set; press. Repeat to make a total of six strip sets.

2. Subcut strip sets into the following units referring to Figure 1: five 5½" x 5½" B, four 5½" x 10½" C, eight 5½" x 15½" D and one 5½" x 25½" E. ***Note:*** *Subcut beginning with the longest strips and continuing to the shortest strips to make best use of the strip sets.*

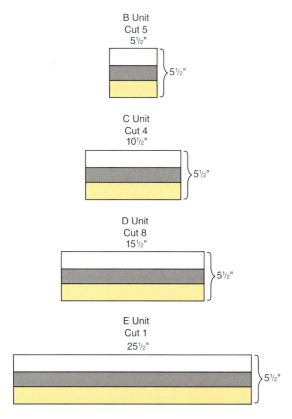

B Unit
Cut 5
5½"
5½"

C Unit
Cut 4
10½"
5½"

D Unit
Cut 8
15½"
5½"

E Unit
Cut 1
25½"
5½"

Figure 1

3. Arrange and join the units and the A squares in seven vertical rows; press.

4. Join the rows to complete the quilt center; press.

5. Sew F strips to opposite long sides and G strips to the top and bottom of the quilt center; press.

6. Join the H/I strips on the short ends to make a long strip; press. Subcut strip into two each 4½" x 43½" H strips and 4½" x 46½" I strips.

7. Sew the H strips to opposite long sides and I strips to the top and bottom of the quilt center; press.

8. Join the J/K strips on the short ends to make a long strip; press. Subcut strip into two each 1½" x 51½" J strips and 1½" x 48½" K strips.

9. Sew the J strips to opposite long sides and K strips to the top and bottom of the quilt center to complete the quilt top; press.

10. Create a quilt sandwich referring to Quilting Basics on page 44.

11. Quilt as desired.

12. Bind referring to Quilting Basics on page 44 to finish. ●

Inspiration

"Of course the inspiration for this quilt was the challenge to make a quilt top out of three yards of fabric! Then the actual quilt inspired me, and I got excited about the endless possibilities this design offered. How often do we as quilters buy a piece of fabric simply because we love it. We're sure we can figure out how to use it in a quilt later. This is that quilt."

—Julie Weaver

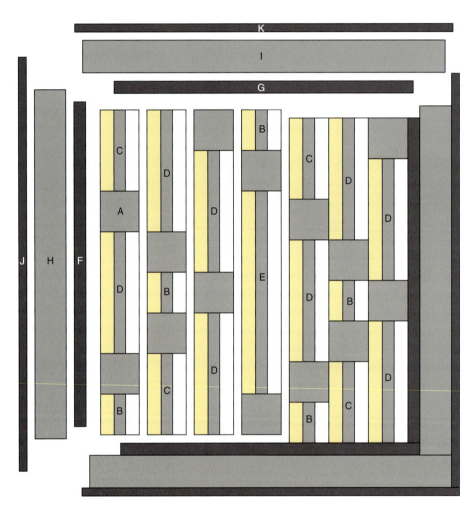

How Does Your Garden Grow?
Assembly Diagram 48" x 53"

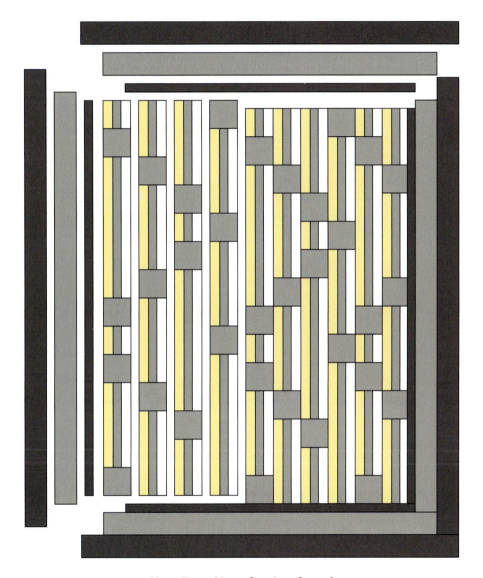

How Does Your Garden Grow?
Alternate-Size Assembly Diagram 69" x 89"
Make a twin-size version of this easy-to-stitch quilt by adding
more units and squares to make longer rows and add more rows
to make a wider quilt. Add wider outer borders to balance the
scale of the finished quilt.

Nightfire Bed Runner

Almost-solid fabrics add modern visual appeal to this bold yet traditional version of the Courthouse Steps block.

Designed & Quilted by Tricia Lynn Maloney

Skill Level
Confident Beginner

Project Note
The yardages listed include just a little extra fabric for straightening. We advise you to purchase extra to allow for straightening your fabric before and during the cutting process if your fabric supplier does not do so when cutting your yardage.

Specifications
Bed Runner Size: 84" x 24"
Block Size: 12" x 12" finished
Number of Blocks: 14

Materials
- ⅝ yard binding fabric
- 1 yard black tonal
- 1 yard red tonal
- 1 yard gray solid
- Backing to size
- Batting to size
- Thread
- Basic sewing tools and supplies

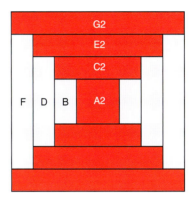

Red Courthouse Steps
12" x 12" Finished Block
Make 7

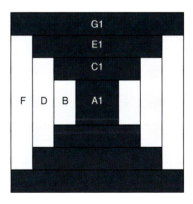

Black Courthouse Steps
12" x 12" Finished Block
Make 7

Cutting

From binding fabric:
- Cut 6 (2¼" by fabric width) binding strips.

From black tonal:
- Cut 1 (3½" by fabric width) strip.
  Subcut strip into 7 (3½") A1 squares.
- Cut 12 (2" by fabric width) strips.
  Subcut 3 strips into 14 (2" x 6½") C1 rectangles.
  Subcut 4 strips into 14 (2" x 9½") E1 rectangles
  Subcut 5 strips into 14 (2" x 12½") G1 rectangles.

From red tonal:
- Cut 1 (3½" by fabric width) strip.
  Subcut strip into 7 (3½") A2 squares.
- Cut 12 (2" by fabric width) strips.
  Subcut 3 strips into 14 (2" x 6½") C2 rectangles.
  Subcut 4 strips into 14 (2" x 9½") E2 rectangles.
  Subcut 5 strips into 14 (2" x 12½") G2 rectangles.

From gray solid:
- Cut 15 (2" by fabric width) strips.
  Subcut 3 strips into 28 (2" x 3½") B rectangles.
  Subcut 5 strips into 28 (2" x 6½") D rectangles.
  Subcut 7 strips into 28 (2" x 9½") F rectangles.

Inspiration

"I love to start a project with a traditional block design and then make it modern with fabric and repetition of geometric shapes."

—Tricia Lynn Maloney

Completing the Blocks

1. Select one A1 square and two each C1, E1 G1, B, D and F rectangles to complete one Black Courthouse Steps block.

2. Sew a B rectangle to opposite sides of A1 as shown in Figure 1; press.

Figure 1

3. Sew a C1 rectangle to the top and bottom of the pieced unit as shown in Figure 2; press.

Figure 2

4. Continue adding pieces in alphabetical order to complete one Black Courthouse Steps block referring to Figure 3 for positioning of rectangles, pressing after adding each set of rectangles.

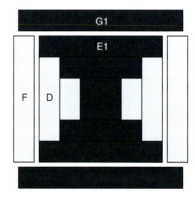

Figure 3

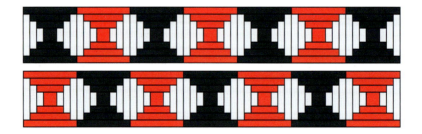

Nightfire Bed Runner
Assembly Diagram 84" x 24"

5. Repeat steps 1–4 to complete a total of seven Black Courthouse Steps blocks.

6. Repeat steps 1–4 with the A2 squares and C2 E2, G2, B, D and F rectangles to complete seven Red Courthouse Steps blocks referring to the block drawing.

Completing the Bed Runner

Refer to the Assembly Diagram for positioning of pieces for all steps.

1. Arrange and join three Black Courthouse Steps blocks with four Red Courthouse Steps blocks to make a row; press.

2. Arrange and join three Red Courthouse Steps blocks with four Black Courthouse Steps blocks to make a row; press.

3. Join the rows to complete the bed runner top; press.

4. Create a quilt sandwich referring to Quilting Basics on page 44.

5. Quilt as desired.

6. Bind referring to Quilting Basics on page 44 to finish. ●

Here's a Tip

Taking the extra time to pin blocks together when you need to match multiple seams will help ensure that everything lines up perfectly.

Beaches Wall Hanging

Add a bit of simple fusible appliqué and change the entire look of a traditional block. This wall hanging looks much harder than it actually is. No one will guess it has faux curves.

Designed & Quilted by Jennifer Schifano Thomas

Skill Level
Intermediate

Specifications
Wall Hanging Size: 26" x 26"
Block Size: 8" x 8" finished
Number of Blocks: 9

Materials
- ¼ yard green batik
- ⅓ yard binding fabric
- ½ yard cream batik
- ⅝ yard turquoise batik
- ⅝ yard purple batik
- Backing to size
- Batting to size
- Thread
- 1 yard fusible web
- Basic sewing tools and supplies

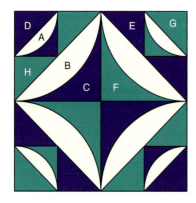

Beaches
8" x 8" Finished Block
Make 9

Cutting
Prepare templates for the A and B pieces using patterns given; cut from the cream batik as directed on each piece and in the instructions.

From green batik:
- Cut 4 (1½" by fabric width) strips.
  Trim strips to make 2 (1½" x 24½") I strips and 2 (1½" x 26½") J strips.

From binding fabric:
- Cut 3 (2¼" by fabric width) binding strips.

From turquoise batik:
- Cut 1 (2½" by fabric width) strip.
  Subcut strip into 16 (2½") G squares.
- Cut 2 (4⅞" by fabric width) strips.
  Subcut strips into 9 (4⅞") F squares and 2 (2½") G squares (18 total). Cut each F square in half on 1 diagonal to make 18 F triangles.
- Cut 2 (2⅞" by fabric width) strips.
  Subcut strips into 18 (2⅞") squares. Cut each square in half on 1 diagonal to make 36 H triangles.

From purple batik:
- Cut 1 (2½" by fabric width) strip.
  Subcut strip into 16 (2½") D squares.
- Cut 2 (4⅞" by fabric width) strips.
  Subcut strips into 9 (4⅞") C squares and 2 (2½") D squares (18 total). Cut each C square in half on 1 diagonal to make 18 C triangles.
- Cut 2 (2⅞" by fabric width) strips.
  Subcut strips into 18 (2⅞") squares. Cut each square in half on 1 diagonal to make 36 E triangles.

Completing the Blocks

1. Referring to number to cut on patterns, trace the A and B shapes onto the paper side of the fusible web leaving ⅛"–¼" between pieces; cut out pieces leaving a margin around each one.

2. Fuse shapes to the wrong side of the cream batik; cut out shapes on traced lines. Remove paper backing.

3. Select two each C, D, G and F pieces and four each A, B, E and H pieces to complete one Beaches block.

4. Sew an H triangle to two adjacent sides of D to complete a purple corner unit as shown in Figure 1; press. Repeat to make a second unit.

Figure 1

5. Repeat step 4 with E triangles and G squares to make two turquoise corner units, again referring to Figure 1.

6. Sew a C triangle to a purple corner unit and an F triangle to a turquoise corner unit to make two each purple and turquoise block quarters as shown in Figure 2; press.

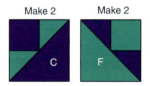

Figure 2

Inspiration

"The 'it takes three' concept inspired me to not only create a quilt using three yards of fabric, but also with three of my favorite quilt elements— batiks, curves and fusible appliqué."

—Jennifer Schifano Thomas

7. Arrange and join the block quarters to complete one block unit referring to Figure 3; press.

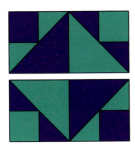

Figure 3

8. Arrange and fuse the A pieces to the D and G squares referring to Figure 4, leaving a ¼" seam allowance at each end.

Figure 4

9. Repeat step 8 with the B pieces on C and F referring to Figure 5.

Figure 5

10. Using thread to match A and B pieces, machine-appliqué pieces in place using your favorite machine-appliqué stitch to complete the Beaches block.

11. Repeat steps 3–10 to complete a total of nine Beaches blocks.

Completing the Wall Hanging

Refer to the Placement Diagram for positioning of pieces for all steps.

1. Join three blocks to make a row; press. Repeat to make a total of three rows.

2. Join the rows to complete the quilt center; press.

3. Sew I strips to the top and bottom, and J strips to opposite sides of the quilt center to complete the quilt top; press.

4. Create a quilt sandwich referring to Quilting Basics on page 44.

5. Quilt as desired.

6. Bind referring to Quilting Basics on page 44 to finish. ●

Here's a Tip

Stitch slowly while zigzagging the edges of patches A and B. Lift your presser foot to pivot often for a smooth-edge treatment.

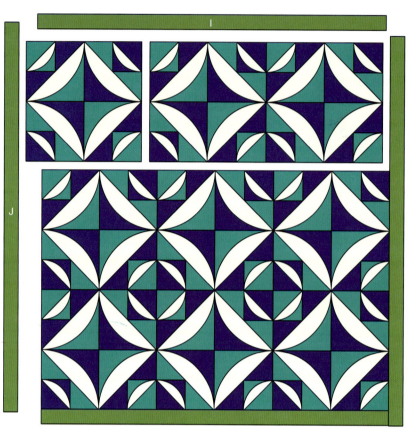

Beaches Wall Hanging
Assembly Diagram 26" x 26"

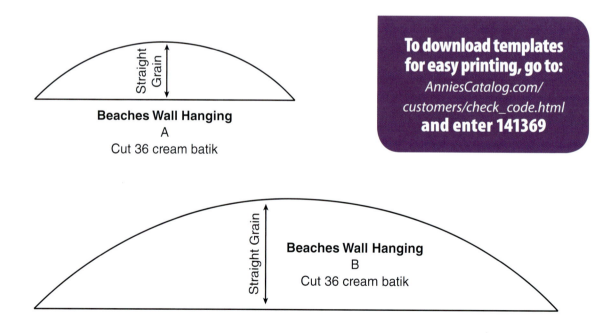

Beaches Wall Hanging
A
Cut 36 cream batik

Beaches Wall Hanging
B
Cut 36 cream batik

To download templates for easy printing, go to:
AnniesCatalog.com/ customers/check_code.html
and enter 141369

Straight Grain

Straight Grain

Raw-Edge Fusible Appliqué

One of the easiest ways to appliqué is the fusible-web method. Paper-backed fusible web motifs are fused to the wrong side of fabric, cut out and then fused to a foundation fabric and stitched in place by hand or machine. You can use this method for raw- or turned-edge appliqué.

1. If the appliqué motif is directional, it should be reversed for raw-edge fusible appliqué. If doing several identical appliqué motifs, trace reversed motif shapes onto template material to make reusable templates.

2. Use templates or trace the appliqué motif shapes onto paper side of paper-backed fusible web. Leave at least ½" between shapes. Cut out shapes leaving a margin around traced lines.

3. Follow manufacturer's instructions and fuse shapes to wrong side of fabric as indicated on pattern for color and number to cut.

4. Cut out appliqué shapes on traced lines and remove paper backing from fusible web.

5. Again following manufacturer's instructions, arrange and fuse pieces on the foundation fabric referring to appliqué motif included in pattern.

6. Hand- or machine-stitch around edges. ***Note:*** *Position a light- to medium-weight stabilizer behind the appliqué motif to keep the fabric from puckering during machine stitching.* Some stitch possibilities are satin, zigzag, blanket or running stitch.

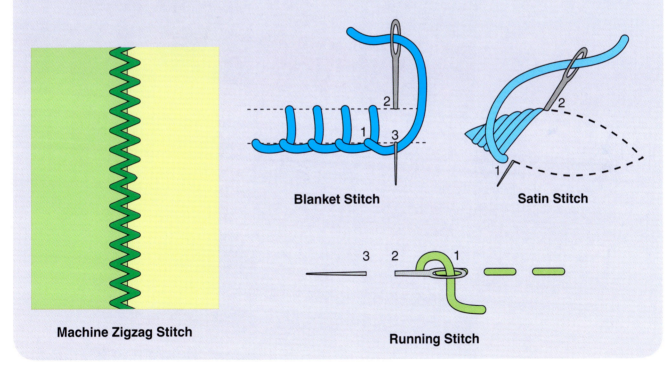

Blanket Stitch

Satin Stitch

Machine Zigzag Stitch

Running Stitch

Star Stomp

Gather your bright and fun fabrics and do the Star Stomp!

Designed & Quilted by Tricia Lynn Maloney

Skill Level

Confident Beginner

Specifications

Quilt Size: 44" x 44"
Block Size: 8" x 8" finished
Number of Blocks: 13

Materials

- 4 assorted fat quarters
- ½ yard binding fabric
- ⅞ yard black floral
- 1⅛ yards white print
- Backing to size
- Batting to size
- Thread
- Basic sewing tools and supplies

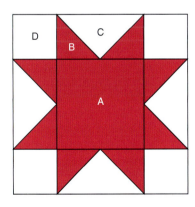

Sawtooth Star
8" x 8" Finished Block
Make 13

Cutting

From 1 fat quarter:

- Cut 1 (4½" x 21") strip.
    Subcut strip into 4 (4½") A squares.
- Cut 3 (2⅞" x 21") strips.
    Subcut strips into 16 (2⅞") squares. Cut each square
        in half on 1 diagonal to make 32 B triangles.

From 3 remaining fat quarters:

- Cut 1 (4½" x 21") strip each fabric.
    Subcut strips into 3 (4½") A squares each fabric.
- Cut 2 (2⅞" x 21") strips each fabric.
    Subcut strips into 12 (2⅞") squares each fabric.
        Cut each square in half on 1 diagonal to make
        24 B triangles each fabric.

From binding fabric:

- Cut 5 (2¼" by fabric width) binding strips.

From black floral:

- Cut 3 (8½" by fabric width) strips.
    Subcut strips into 12 (8½") E squares and
        4 (2½") G squares.

From white print:

- Cut 2 (5¼" by fabric width) strips.
    Subcut strips into 13 (5¼") C squares and 4 (2½")
        D squares. Cut each C square on both diagonals
        to make 52 C triangles.
- Cut 7 (2½" by fabric width) strips.
    Trim 4 strips to make 4 (2½" x 40½") F strips.
    Subcut the 3 remaining strips into 48 (2½")
        D squares (52 total).

Completing the Blocks

1. To complete one Sawtooth Star block, select one A square and eight matching B triangles with four each C triangles and D squares.

2. Sew B to each short side of C to make a side unit as shown in Figure 1; press. Repeat to make a total of four side units.

Side Unit
Make 4

Figure 1

3. Sew a side unit to opposite sides of A to make the center row as shown in Figure 2; press.

Figure 2

4. Sew a D square to each end of each remaining side unit to make the top and bottom rows referring to Figure 3; press.

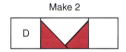

Make 2

Figure 3

5. Sew the top and bottom rows to the center row to complete one Sawtooth Star block referring to Figure 4; press.

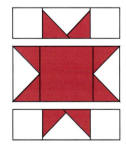

Figure 4

6. Repeat steps 1–5 to complete a total of 13 Sawtooth Star blocks.

Completing the Quilt

Refer to the Assembly Diagram for positioning of pieces for all steps.

1. Arrange and join two E squares with three Sawtooth Star blocks to make an X row; press. Repeat to make a total of three X rows.

2. Arrange and join two Sawtooth Star blocks with three E squares to make a Y row; press. Repeat to make a second Y row.

3. Arrange and join the X and Y rows to complete the quilt center; press.

4. Sew an F strip to opposite sides of the quilt center; press.

5. Sew a G square to each end of each remaining F strip and sew these strips to the top and bottom of the quilt center to complete the quilt top; press.

6. Create a quilt sandwich referring to Quilting Basics on page 44.

7. Quilt as desired.

8. Bind referring to Quilting Basics on page 44 to finish. ●

Here's a Tip

Don't be afraid to flaunt your large prints.

Inspiration

"I am always inspired by beautiful fabrics paired with traditional quilt block designs, and you can't get more traditional than a Sawtooth Star."

—Tricia Lynn Maloney

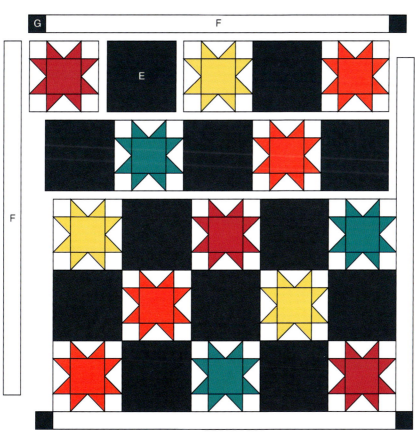

Star Stomp
Assembly Diagram 44" x 44"

Slightly Askew

Construct eight of these fast and easy blocks, and you're almost finished.

Design by Lyn Brown
Quilted by Jami Goto

Skill Level
Confident Beginner

Project Note
The yardages listed include just a little extra fabric for straightening. We advise you to purchase extra to allow for straightening your fabric before and during the cutting process if your fabric supplier does not do so when cutting your yardage.

Specifications
Quilt Size: 45" x 61"
Block Size: 16" x 12" finished
Number of Blocks: 8

Materials
- ⅓ yard dark violet batik
- ⅓ yard light violet batik
- ⅓ yard dark pink batik
- ½ yard binding fabric
- 1 yard gray batik
- 1 yard light pink batik
- Backing to size
- Batting to size
- Thread
- Basic sewing tools and supplies

Cutting

From dark violet batik:
- Cut 1 (8½" by width of fabric) strip.

From light violet batik:
- Cut 1 (8½" by width of fabric) strip.

From dark pink batik:
- Cut 1 (8½" by width of fabric) strip.

From binding fabric:
- Cut 6 (2¼" by fabric width) binding strips.

From gray batik:
- Cut 5 (2½" by fabric width) E/F strips.
    Subcut 2 strips to 2½" x 32½" E strips.
- Cut 2 (4½" by fabric width) strips.
- Cut 4 (2½" by fabric width) strips.

From light pink batik:
- Cut 1 (8½" by fabric width) strip.
- Cut 5 (5" by fabric width) G/H strips.
    Trim 2 strips to make 2 (5" x 36½") G strips.

Inspiration

"Believe it or not, this quilt was inspired by the brickwork outside my local big-box–chain discount store. I loved the play of large and small bricks, and chose to keep the patches practically life sized. Twisting and mirror-imaging the simple blocks made a dynamic design."

—Lyn Brown

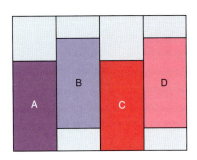

Block 1
16" x 12" Finished Block
Make 2

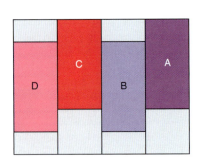

Block 3
16" x 12" Finished Block
Make 2

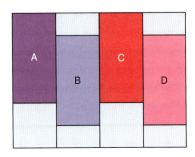

Block 2
16" x 12" Finished Block
Make 2

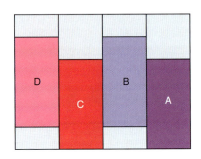

Block 4
16" x 12" Finished Block
Make 2

Completing the Blocks

1. Sew a 4½"-wide gray strip to the 8½"-wide dark violet strip along length to make a strip set; press. Subcut strip set into eight 4½" x 12½" A units as shown in Figure 1.

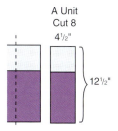

A Unit
Cut 8
4½"
12½"

Figure 1

2. Sew the 8½"-wide light violet strip between two 2½"-wide gray strips along length to make a strip set; press. Subcut strip set into eight 4½" x 12½" B units as shown in Figure 2.

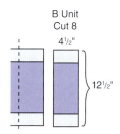

B Unit
Cut 8
4½"
12½"

Figure 2

3. Sew a 4½"-wide gray strip to the 8½"-wide dark pink strip along length to make a strip set; press. Subcut strip set into eight 4½" x 12½" C units as shown in Figure 3.

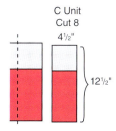

C Unit
Cut 8
4½"
12½"

Figure 3

4. Sew the 8½"-wide light pink strip between two 2½"-wide gray strips along length to make a strip set; press. Subcut strip set into eight 4½" x 12½" D units as shown in Figure 4.

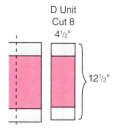

D Unit
Cut 8
4½"
12½"

Figure 4

5. Select one each A, B, C and D unit and join as shown in Figure 5 to complete one Block 1; press. Repeat to make a second block.

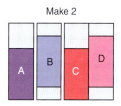

Make 2

Figure 5

6. Repeat step 5 turning the A and C units as shown in Figure 6 to complete two Block 2's; press.

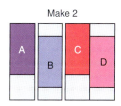

Make 2

Figure 6

7. Repeat step 5 to make two each Blocks 3 and 4 rearranging the units as shown in Figure 7; press.

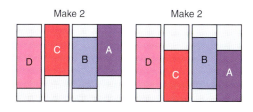

Make 2   Make 2

Figure 7

Completing the Quilt

Refer to the Assembly Diagram for positioning of pieces for all steps.

1. Arrange and join the blocks in four rows of two blocks each; press.

2. Join the rows to complete the quilt center; press.

3. Sew the E strips to the top and bottom of the quilt center; press.

4. Join the F strips on the short ends to make a long strip; press. Subcut strip into two 2½" x 52½" F strips.

5. Sew the F strips to opposite long sides of the quilt center; press.

6. Sew the G strips to the top and bottom of the bordered quilt center; press.

7. Join the H strips on the short ends to make a long strip; press. Subcut strip into two 5" x 61½" H strips.

Slightly Askew
Assembly Diagram 45" x 61"

8. Sew the H strips to opposite long sides of the bordered quilt center to complete the quilt top; press.

9. Create a quilt sandwich referring to Quilting Basics on page 44.

10. Quilt as desired.

11. Bind referring to Quilting Basics on page 44 to finish. ●

Here's a Tip

Large patches, simple piecing and a trick of the mirror make quick-pieced blocks dance across this quilt.

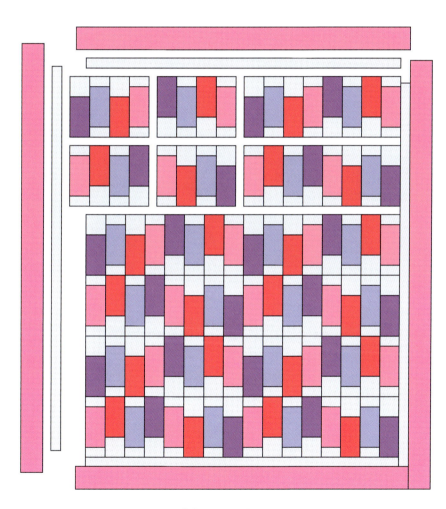

Slightly Askew
Alternate-Size Assembly Diagram 77" x 85"
Add 2 blocks to the width and 2 to the
length to make a twin-size quilt.

Baby Bows

Easy dimensional piecing and bright fabrics are sure to please any little one. This is ideal for a make-ahead shower gift.

Designed & Quilted by Bev Getschel

Skill Level

Beginner

Specifications

Quilt Size: 42" x 42"
Block Size: 6" x 6" finished
Number of Blocks: 36

Materials

- 1 fat quarter each of the following: red and blue tonals, and green, yellow, blue and orange prints
- ½ yard binding fabric
- ½ yard coordinating stripe (43" usable width)
- ¾ yard white print
- Backing to size
- Batting to size
- Thread
- ⅔ yard fusible web
- Basic sewing tools and supplies

Cutting

Prepare a template for the circle using pattern given; cut from the red and blue tonal fat quarters as directed on the piece and in the instructions.

From the green, yellow, blue and orange print fat quarters:

- Cut 5 (3½" x 21") strips from each fabric.
  Subcut strips into 27 (3½") A squares each fabric (108 total).

From binding fabric:

- Cut 5 (2¼" by fabric width) binding strips.

From coordinating stripe:

- Cut 4 (3½" by fabric width) strips.
  Trim strips to make 2 (3½" x 36½") C strips and 2 (3½" x 42½") D strips.

From white print:

- Cut 6 (3½" by fabric width) strips.
  Subcut strips into 72 (3½") B squares.

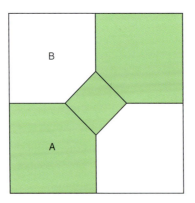

Bow Tie
6" x 6" Finished Block
Make 36

It Takes Three

Completing the Blocks

1. Select two B squares and three same-fabric A squares to complete one Bow Tie block.

2. Fold one A square in half with wrong sides together to make a rectangle. Do not press.

3. Sandwich the folded A piece between one A and one B square, right sides together and matching top and side raw edges; stitch together along the right edge referring to Figure 1.

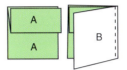

Figure 1

4. Open the stitched unit and fold the A and B squares away from the folded A square as shown in Figure 2.

Figure 2

5. Place the short unstitched edge of the folded A square between the second pair of A and B squares, alternating the positioning of the squares from the opposite end as shown in Figure 3.

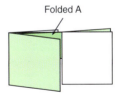

Figure 3

6. Stitch and open the unit as in steps 3 and 4 and referring to Figure 4.

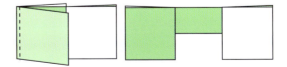

Figure 4

7. Open the folded A pocket and spread apart with your fingers, pulling the other A and B squares together; match the seams and align the raw edges of the A pocket with the edges of the A-B unit referring to Figure 5.

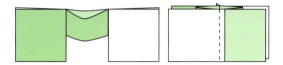

Figure 5

8. Stitch across the long edge; open and press the A pocket flat and the seams in opposite directions to complete one Bow Tie block referring to Figure 6.

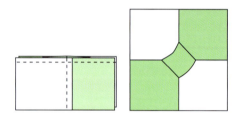

Figure 6

9. Repeat steps 1–8 to complete a total of 36 Bow Tie blocks as shown in Figure 7.

Make 9 each color

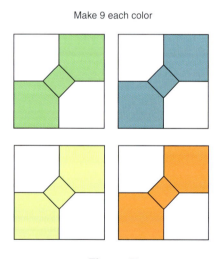

Figure 7

Completing the Quilt

Refer to the Placement Diagram for positioning of pieces for steps 2–8.

1. Arrange and join three each green and blue blocks to make a row as shown in Figure 8; press. Repeat to make a total of three rows. Repeat with three each yellow and orange blocks to make three rows, again referring to Figure 8.

Make 3

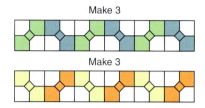

Make 3

Figure 8

2. Arrange and join the rows to complete the pieced center; press.

3. Sew C strips to the top and bottom, and D strips to opposite sides of the pieced center; press.

4. Trace 25 circle shapes onto the paper side of the fusible web, leaving ⅛" between pieces. Cut out circles, leaving a margin around each one.

5. Fuse 16 circles to the wrong side of the red tonal and 9 circles to the wrong side of the blue tonal. Cut out circles on traced lines; remove paper backing.

6. Center and fuse the circles in the B square sections.

7. Using thread to match fabric and your favorite machine-appliqué stitch, sew circles in place all around to complete the quilt top.

8. Create a quilt sandwich referring to Quilting Basics on page 44.

9. Quilt as desired.

10. Bind referring to Quilting Basics on page 44 to finish. ●

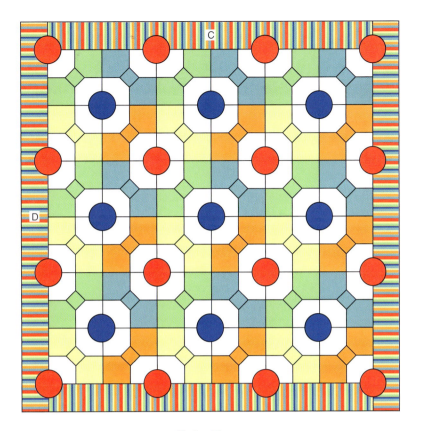

Baby Bows
Placement Diagram 42" x 42"

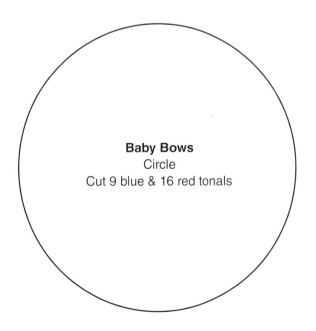

Baby Bows
Circle
Cut 9 blue & 16 red tonals

Quilting Basics

The following is a reference guide. For more information, consult a comprehensive quilting book.

Always:

- Read through the entire pattern before you begin your project.
- Purchase quality, 100 percent cotton fabrics.
- When considering prewashing, do so with ALL of the fabrics being used. Generally, prewashing is not required in quilting.
- Use ¼" seam allowance for all stitching unless otherwise instructed.
- Use a short-to-medium stitch length.
- Make sure your seams are accurate.

Quilting Tools & Supplies

- Rotary cutter and mat
- Scissors for paper and fabric
- Non-slip quilting rulers
- Marking tools
- Sewing machine
- Sewing machine feet:
    - ¼" seaming foot (for piecing)
    - Walking or even-feed foot (for piecing or quilting)
    - Darning or free-motion foot (for free-motion quilting)
- Quilting hand-sewing needles
- Straight pins
- Curved safety pins for basting
- Seam ripper
- Iron and ironing surface

Basic Techniques

Appliqué

Fusible Appliqué

All templates in *Quilter's World* are reversed for use with this technique.

1. Trace the instructed number of templates ¼" apart onto the paper side of paper-backed fusible web. Cut apart the templates, leaving a margin around each, and fuse to the wrong side of the fabric following fusible web manufacturer's instructions.

2. Cut the appliqué pieces out on the traced lines, remove paper backing and fuse to the background referring to the appliqué motif given.

3. Finish appliqué raw edges with a straight, satin, blanket, zigzag or blind-hem machine stitch with matching or invisible thread.

Turned-Edge Appliqué

1. Trace the printed reversed templates onto template plastic. Flip the template over and mark as the right side.

2. Position the template, right side up, on the right side of fabric and lightly trace, spacing images ½" apart. Cut apart, leaving a ¼" margin around the traced lines.

3. Clip curves and press edges ¼" to the wrong side around the appliqué shape.

4. Referring to the appliqué motif, pin or baste appliqué shapes to the background.

5. Hand-stitch shapes in place using a blind stitch and thread to match or machine-stitch using a short blind hemstitch and either matching or invisible thread.

Borders

Most *Quilter's World* patterns give an exact size to cut borders. You may check those sizes by comparing them to the horizontal and vertical center measurements of your quilt top.

Straight Borders

1. Mark the centers of the side borders and quilt top sides.

2. Stitch borders to quilt top sides with right sides together and matching raw edges and center marks using a ¼" seam. Press seams toward borders.

3. Repeat with top and bottom border lengths.

Mitered Borders

1. Add at least twice the border width to the border lengths instructed to cut.

2. Center and sew the side borders to the quilt, beginning and ending stitching ¼" from the quilt corner and backstitching (Figure 1). Repeat with the top and bottom borders.

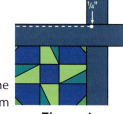

Figure 1

3. Fold and pin quilt right sides together at a 45-degree angle on one corner (Figure 2). Place a straightedge along the fold and lightly mark a line across the border ends.

Figure 2

4. Stitch along the line, backstitching to secure. Trim seam to ¼" and press open (Figure 3).

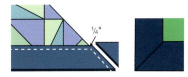

Figure 3

Quilt Backing & Batting

We suggest that you cut your backing and batting 8" larger than the finished quilt-top size. If preparing the backing from standard-width fabrics, remove the selvages and sew two or three lengths together; press seams open. If using 108"-wide fabric, trim to size on the straight grain of the fabric.

Prepare batting the same size as your backing. You can purchase prepackaged sizes or battings by the yard and trim to size.

Quilting

1. Press quilt top on both sides and trim all loose threads.

2. Make a quilt sandwich by layering the backing right side down, batting and quilt top centered right side up on flat surface and smooth out. Pin or baste layers together to hold.

3. Mark quilting design on quilt top and quilt as desired by hand or machine. *Note: If you are sending your quilt to a professional quilter, contact them for specifics about preparing your quilt for quilting.*

4. When quilting is complete, remove pins or basting. Trim batting and backing edges even with raw edges of quilt top.

Binding the Quilt

1. Join binding strips on short ends with diagonal seams to make one long strip; trim seams to ¼" and press seams open (Figure 4).

2. Fold 1" of one short end to wrong side and press. Fold the binding strip in half with wrong sides together along length, again referring to Figure 4; press.

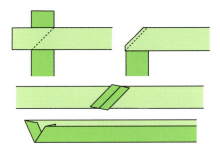

Figure 4

3. Starting about 3" from the folded short end, sew binding to quilt top edges, matching raw edges and using a ¼" seam. Stop stitching ¼" from corner and backstitch (Figure 5).

Figure 5

4. Fold binding up at a 45-degree angle to seam and then down even with quilt edges, forming a pleat at corner, referring to Figure 6.

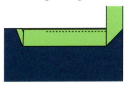

Figure 6

5. Resume stitching from corner edge as shown in Figure 6, down quilt side, backstitching ¼" from next corner. Repeat, mitering all corners, stitching to within 3" of starting point.

6. Trim binding end long enough to tuck inside starting end and complete stitching (Figure 7).

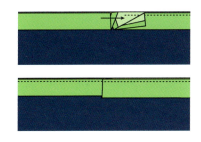

Figure 7

7. Fold binding to quilt back and stitch in place by hand or machine to complete your quilt.

Quilting Terms

- **Appliqué:** Adding fabric motifs to a foundation fabric by hand or machine (see Appliqué section of Basic Techniques).

- **Basting:** This temporarily secures layers of quilting materials together with safety pins, thread or a spray adhesive in preparation for quilting the layers.

  Use a long, straight stitch to hand- or machine-stitch one element to another holding the elements in place during construction and usually removed after construction.

- **Batting:** An insulating material made in a variety of fiber contents that is used between the quilt top and back to provide extra warmth and loft.

- **Binding:** A finishing strip of fabric sewn to the outer raw edges of a quilt to cover them.

  Straight-grain binding strips, cut on the crosswise straight grain of the fabric (see Straight & Bias Grain Lines illustration on page 46), are commonly used.

  Bias binding strips are cut at a 45-degree angle to the straight grain of the fabric. They are used when binding is being added to curved edges.

- **Block:** The basic quilting unit that is repeated to complete the quilt's design composition. Blocks can be pieced, appliquéd or solid and are usually square or rectangular in shape.
- **Border:** The frame of a quilt's central design used to visually complete the design and give the eye a place to rest.
- **Fabric Grain:** The fibers that run either parallel (lengthwise grain) or perpendicular (crosswise grain) to the fabric selvage are straight grain.

  Bias is any diagonal line between the lengthwise or crosswise grain. At these angles the fabric is less stable and stretches easily. The true bias of a woven fabric is a 45-degree angle between the lengthwise and crosswise grain lines.

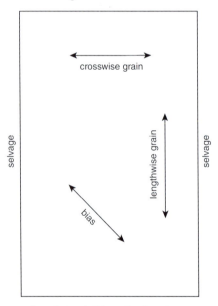

Straight & Bias Grain Lines

- **Mitered Corners:** Matching borders or turning bindings at a 45-degree angle at corners.
- **Patchwork:** A general term for the completed blocks or quilts that are made from smaller shapes sewn together.
- **Pattern:** This may refer to the design of a fabric or to the written instructions for a particular quilt design.

- **Piecing:** The act of sewing smaller pieces and/or units of a block or quilt together.

  Paper or foundation piecing is sewing fabric to a paper or cloth foundation in a certain order.

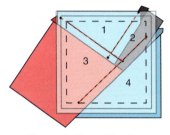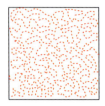

Foundation Piecing

  String or chain piecing is sewing pieces together in a continuous string without clipping threads between sections.

String or Chain Piecing

Pressing: Pressing is the process of placing the iron on the fabric, lifting it off the fabric and placing it down in another location to flatten seams or crease fabric without sliding the iron across the fabric.

  Quilters do not usually use steam when pressing, since it can easily distort fabric shapes.

  Generally, seam allowances are pressed toward the darker fabric in quilting so that they do not show through the lighter fabric.

  Seams are pressed in opposite directions where seams are being joined to allow seams to butt against each other and to distribute bulk.

  Seams are pressed open when multiple seams come together in one place.

  If you have a question about pressing direction, consult a comprehensive quilting guide for guidance.
- **Quilt (noun):** A sandwich of two layers of fabric with a third insulating material between them that is then stitched together with the edges covered or bound.

- **Quilt (verb):** Stitching several layers of fabric materials together with a decorative design. Stippling, cross-hatch, channel, in-the-ditch, free-motion, allover and meandering are all terms for quilting designs.

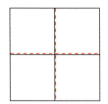

Meandering   **Stitch-in-the-ditch**

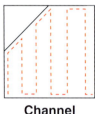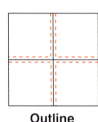

Channel   **Outline**

- **Quilt Sandwich:** A layer of insulating material between a quilt's top and back fabric.
- **Rotary Cutting:** Using a rotary cutting blade and straightedge to cut fabric.
- **Sashing:** Strips of fabric sewn between blocks to separate or set off the designs.
- **Subcut:** A second cutting of rotary-cut strips that makes the basic shapes used in block and quilt construction.
- **Template:** A pattern made from a sturdy material which is then used to cut shapes for patchwork and appliqué quilting.

Quilting Skill Levels

- **Beginner:** A quilter who has been introduced to the basics of cutting, piecing and assembling a quilt top and is working to master these skills. Someone who has the knowledge of how to sandwich, quilt and bind a quilt, but may not have necessarily accomplished the task yet.

- **Confident Beginner:** A quilter who has pieced and assembled several quilt tops and is comfortable with the process, and is now ready to move on to more challenging techniques and projects using at least two different techniques.

- **Intermediate:** A quilter who is comfortable with most quilting techniques and has a good understanding for design, color and the whole process. A quilter who is experienced in paper piecing, bias piecing and projects involving multiple techniques. Someone who is confident in making fabric selections other than those listed in the pattern.

- **Advanced:** A quilter who is looking for a challenging design. Someone who knows she or he can make any type of quilt. Someone who has the skills to read, comprehend and complete a pattern, and is willing to take on any technique. A quilter who is comfortable in her or his skills and has the ability to select fabric suited to the project. ●

METRIC CONVERSION CHARTS

Metric Conversions

Canada/U.S. Measurement		Multiplied by		Metric Measurement
yards	x	.9144	=	metres (m)
yards	x	91.44	=	centimetres (cm)
inches	x	2.54	=	centimetres (cm)
inches	x	25.40	=	millimetres (mm)
inches	x	.0254	=	metres (m)

Canada/U.S. Measurement		Multiplied by		Metric Measurement
centimetres	x	.3937	=	inches
metres	x	1.0936	=	yards

Standard Equivalents

Canada/U.S. Measurement		Metric Measurement		
⅛ inch	=	3.20 mm	=	0.32 cm
¼ inch	=	6.35 mm	=	0.635 cm
⅜ inch	=	9.50 mm	=	0.95 cm
½ inch	=	12.70 mm	=	1.27 cm
⅝ inch	=	15.90 mm	=	1.59 cm
¾ inch	=	19.10 mm	=	1.91 cm
⅞ inch	=	22.20 mm	=	2.22 cm
1 inches	=	25.40 mm	=	2.54 cm
⅛ yard	=	11.43 cm	=	0.11 m
¼ yard	=	22.86 cm	=	0.23 m
⅜ yard	=	34.29 cm	=	0.34 m
½ yard	=	45.72 cm	=	0.46 m
⅝ yard	=	57.15 cm	=	0.57 m
¾ yard	=	68.58 cm	=	0.69 m
⅞ yard	=	80.00 cm	=	0.80 m
1 yard	=	91.44 cm	=	0.91 m
1⅛ yards	=	102.87 cm	=	1.03 m
1¼ yards	=	114.30 cm	=	1.14 m

Canada/U.S. Measurement		Metric Measurement		
1⅜ yards	=	125.73 cm	=	1.26 m
1½ yards	=	137.16 cm	=	1.37 m
1⅝ yards	=	148.59 cm	=	1.49 m
1¾ yards	=	160.02 cm	=	1.60 m
1⅞ yards	=	171.44 cm	=	1.71 m
2 yards	=	182.88 cm	=	1.83 m
2⅛ yards	=	194.31 cm	=	1.94 m
2¼ yards	=	205.74 cm	=	2.06 m
2⅜ yards	=	217.17 cm	=	2.17 m
2½ yards	=	228.60 cm	=	2.29 m
2⅝ yards	=	240.03 cm	=	2.40 m
2¾ yards	=	251.46 cm	=	2.51 m
2⅞ yards	=	262.88 cm	=	2.63 m
3 yards	=	274.32 cm	=	2.74 m
3⅛ yards	=	285.75 cm	=	2.86 m
3¼ yards	=	297.18 cm	=	2.97 m
3⅜ yards	=	308.61 cm	=	3.09 m
3½ yards	=	320.04 cm	=	3.20 m
3⅝ yards	=	331.47 cm	=	3.31 m
3¾ yards	=	342.90 cm	=	3.43 m
3⅞ yards	=	354.32 cm	=	3.54 m
4 yards	=	365.76 cm	=	3.66 m
4⅛ yards	=	377.19 cm	=	3.77 m
4¼ yards	=	388.62 cm	=	3.89 m
4⅜ yards	=	400.05 cm	=	4.00 m
4½ yards	=	411.48 cm	=	4.11 m
4⅝ yards	=	422.91 cm	=	4.23 m
4¾ yards	=	434.34 cm	=	4.34 m
4⅞ yards	=	445.76 cm	=	4.46 m
5 yards	=	457.20 cm	=	4.57 m

Special Thanks

Please join us in thanking the talented designers whose work is featured in this collection.

Lyn Brown
Slightly Askew, page 32

Bev Getschel
Baby Bows, page 38

Tricia Lynn Maloney
Nightfire Bed Runner, page 19
Star Stomp, page 29

Jennifer Schifano Thomas
Beaches Wall Hanging, page 22

Julie Weaver
Appian Way Bed Runner, page 3
My Shadow, page 9
How Does Your Garden Grow?, page 13

Supplies

We would like to thank the following manufacturers who provided materials to our designers to make sample projects for this book.

Appian Way Bed Runner, page 3: Ladies' Album fabric collection from Moda; Warm & Natural cotton batting from The Warm Company.

My Shadow, page 9: Plum Sweet fabric collection from Moda; Thermore batting from Hobbs.

How Does Your Garden Grow?, page 13: Ophelia fabric collection from Timeless Treasures; Thermore batting from Hobbs.

Nightfire Bed Runner, page 19: Fabrics from Timeless Treasures.

Beaches Wall Hanging, page 22: Fabrics from Island Batik; Warm & White batting from The Warm Company.

Star Stomp, page 29: Fiesta fabric collection; Hobbs 80/20 batting and Essential 100 percent cotton thread all provided by Connecting Threads.

Slightly Askew, page 32: Batiks from Hoffman California Fabrics.

Baby Bows, page 38: A is for Animal fabric collection from Red Rooster Fabrics; Poly-Fil® batting from Fairfield.

 It Takes Three is published by Annie's, 306 East Parr Road, Berne, IN 46711. Printed in USA. Copyright © 2014, 2017 Annie's. All rights reserved. This publication may not be reproduced in part or in whole without written permission from the publisher.

RETAIL STORES: If you would like to carry this pattern book or any other Annie's publications, visit AnniesWSL.com

Every effort has been made to ensure that the instructions in this pattern book are complete and accurate. We cannot, however, take responsibility for human error, typographical mistakes or variations in individual work. Please visit AnniesCustomerCare.com to check for pattern updates.

ISBN: 978-1-57367-379-2

4 5 6 7 8 9